SPINACH DAYS

Johns Hopkins: Poetry and Fiction

John T. Irwin, General Editor

Books by Robert Phillips

SPINACH DAYS

POEMS BY ROBERT PHILLIPS

THE JOHNS HOPKINS UNIVERSITY PRESS | BALTIMORE AND LONDON

*This book has been brought to publication with
the generous assistance of the Albert Dowling Trust.*

The Johns Hopkins University Press
2715 North Charles Street
Baltimore, MD 21218-4363
www.press.jhu.edu

Library of Congress Cataloging-in-
Publication Data will
be found at the end of this book.
A catalog record for this book is available
from the British Library.

ISBN 0-8018-6451-8

This book is for Max Eberts—
wonderful writer, editor, and friend

My salad days,
When I was green in judgment.

— SHAKESPEARE

I should not talk so much about myself
If there were anybody else whom I knew so well.

— THOREAU

Contents

Acknowledgments

Thanks to Mitch Cullin, Max Eberts, Dana Gioia, Rob House, Eric Muirhead, William Jay Smith, Daniel Stern, and Drew Ten Eyck for reading and commenting on many of these poems.

Special thanks to the College of Humanities, Fine Arts and Communication, the University of Houston, who granted me a Faculty Development Leave for the 1997–98 academic year, during which time this book initially took shape.

No thanks to the individual who stole a briefcase out of my car on February 4, 1997, resulting in the loss of the complete manuscript of this book, which has been reconstructed without benefit of computer backup.

Thanks to Allen Gee for word processing and rescue.

The following poems have appeared in a number of journals: *Boulevard*: "Oysters"; *Chelsea*: "No Thanksgiving," "Fifth Season"; *Collegium: The Magazine of the University of Houston*: "After the Crash"; *Connecticut Review*: "Homage to a Nonagenarian," "The Uses of Not"; *Georgetown Review*: "Houston Haiku"; *Gulf Coast*: "The Panic Bird," "The Pillsbury Doughboy Is Alive and Well in Ohio," "603 Cross River Road"; *Helicon Nine*: "Late Reading"; *The Hudson Review*: "Compartments," "I Remember, I Remember," "Letter to My Mother," "Spinach Days," "Trashed"; *Modern Literature Collection Newsletter*: "My Valhalla"; *The New Criterion*: "Things"; *Northeast Corridor*: "Instrument of Choice"; *Ontario Review*: "The Gingerbread House," "Hounds," "Never Date Yourself"; *The Paris Review*: "A Pretty Likeness of the Life," "Cherry Suite," "In Praise of My Prostate," "John Dillinger's Dick," "The Land: A Love Letter," "Say Hello to the Little Woman"; *Reed Magazine*: "Sunday Driver"; *Southern Lights*: "Houston Haiku"; *Tar River Poetry*: "Sonata"; *Western Humanities Review*: "After the Crash," "Farewell to the Blue House," "Found Poems."

"My Valhalla" also appeared in *What Have You Lost?*, an anthology of poems, edited by Naomi Shihab Nye (New York: Greenwillow Books, 1999); and in *For David Ignatow: An Anthology*, edited by Robert Long (East Hampton, N.Y.: Guild Hall/ Canio's Editions, 1994).

Part I

I Remember, I Remember
(poem beginning with two lines by Yehuda Amichai)

The earth drinks people and their loves
like wine, in order to forget.
But I drink wine to remember.

I remember the day at school I thought
I had appendicitis. My father came,
supported me on both sides to the car,

into the doctor's. For that, when Gabriel
blows his horn, may Father be supported
on both sides to Heaven.

I remember the sensation of first love,
like falling down a mine shaft.
But shafts are dark, and all around

me was light, light, light. Her hair
light, and when we locked together
we were a dynamo generating light.

I remember not knowing what I wanted to do
in life. My ambitions scattered like newspapers
on lawns of people out of town,

until I had the right professor for
the right course. Suddenly I was on course
for what I'd do until the day I die.

I remember the day we were wed. In early
morning I walked down Marshall Street,
wanted to proclaim to everyone I met,

"I'm marrying a woman who makes me laugh,
a beautiful woman good as fresh-baked bread,
pure as a beach where no one walks."

I remember the day our son was born,
the longest day and night and day
of my life—imagine how long for her!

When the nurse brought our son to the window,
I was Robinson Crusoe discovering Friday's
footprint: stranger, companion, friend.

I remember, sometimes more than I care to,
the friend I let down unintentionally,
the brothers I hurt through simple silence,

the mother I didn't call often enough when
she was bedridden, weak as water. I even
remember a dog who wanted to play. I didn't.

I remember the day it was confirmed
one of my friends had been telling
lies about me for years—

they cost me friends, a coveted job.
May his tongue be ripped out
and flung to the crows.

I collect memories the way some collect coins.
The memories fade like constellations at dawn.
Until my next glass of wine.

For the Late Great Pennsylvania Station
(1910-1966)

"What is our praise or pride but to imagine
Excellence and try to make it?" the poet asked.
Man made it in Manhattan, a dream of pure glory,
    Ornamented by the eagles of Caesars,
    Walled in creamy gold travertine.

Vaunting Doric columns supported a vaulting
Crystal ceiling one-hundred-fifty feet high,
Waiting room the length of two city blocks,
    Space suitable for history to stretch out legs in.
    Exposed structural steel counterpointed,

Spoke to us of the Modern Age's motion and power,
Sepia murals whispered like Penn's Woods' past.
This was our immense New World temple.
    This was our expansiveness and light,
    Interior vista vast as our continent.

When you arrived there, you knew you knew
You had arrived. It cast long shadows,
Contained the sounds of time, for merely
    Fifty-six years—not even a blink.
    Then it fell to greed,

To demolishers of glory, for a chrome
And plastic sports dome that could have squatted
Anywhere. I recollected Ilion and Babylon,
    Coventry and Dresden—hymns to joy, alas.
    That which man has made, *homo perdidit*.

My Valhalla

Forget the Museum of Natural History,
the Metropolitan or the Smithsonian.
The collection I want to wander in
I call the Valhalla of Lost Things.

The Venus de Milo's arms are here,
she's grown quite attached to them.
I circle Leonardo's sixteen-foot-tall
equestrian statue, never cast, browse

all five-hundred-thousand volumes
of the Alexandrian Library, handle
artifacts of Atlantis. Here are all
the ballads and rondeaux of Villon,

the finished score of the *Unfinished Symphony.*
I read Aristotle's missing chapters
of the *Poetics,* last plays of Euripides,
screen missing reels of Von Stroheim's *Greed,*

hear the famous gap in Nixon's tapes.
There are lost things here so lost,
no one knows they were lost—manuscripts
by the unknown Kafka, far greater

than Kafka's; his best friend obeyed,
shredded every sheet. The cure for cancer
is here: the inventor didn't recognize,
the potion went unpatented . . .

In my museum no guard watches me.
There are no closing times,
it's always free. Here I can see
what no one living has seen, I satisfy

that within me which is not whole.
Here I am curator not of what is,
but of what should have been,
and what should be.

Free Improvisation

Frond leaves litter empty parking lots
    like the day after Palm Sunday,
fronds turned yellow as jaundice.
    Fish tanks leak, cloudy cataracts.
Rust drools down spectator portholes.
    Wooden benches rot through, break.
The new superhighway does not pass by.
    Marineland, Florida, is defunct—

except for dolphins. Deep in the park's heart,
    splashes! A dozen dolphins play.
A lone caretaker takes care of them.
    And three times a day they keep time,
flying high, cartwheeling, showboating,
    hotdogging, up on their tails,
free fins waving at empty seats, smiling at
    routines created all by themselves.

Everywhere the Same
(for Daniel Stern)

Little League in the park afternoons,
the railroad through the bad part of town.
Cities are about the same everywhere.

Love asserts importance Saturday nights,
more important than a mountain or tree.
Little League in the park afternoons.

All Delaware roads wend to Wilmington.
All roads in Germany lead to Ausfarht.
Cities are about the same everywhere.

You go to the empty river to fish.
You wander down to the bar to brag lies.
Little League in parks afternoons.

There's a pool hall where only black men play.
Here's a country club that admits no Jews.
Cities are about the same everywhere—

unless your friends and family are there:
People with your face remember your name.
Sad rapists in the park afternoons.
Cities are about the same everywhere.

Early Lesson

Her mother brought her down
to the laundry room. Picking
through the wicker clothes basket
she explained, "You must separate
the colored from the white."
And they did. Their black maid,
ironing in the corner, nodded.

Gingerbread House

A gingerbread house like the one on the cover
is as much fun to make as to look at,
and you may be as whimsical as you like
with its decoration.
> —*The Cooking of Germany*
> (Time-Life Books, 1969)

The parents assist the children
in assembling the gingerbread house.
Stiff cardboard patterns, spicy cakes
fragrantly baking, fixed young faces.

Windows are cut out with a sharp knife,
shutters and trim outlined with jellybeans.
Parents make sure children don't forget
to make a chimney. A chimney is essential.

How much fun it is! Marshmallow snow,
half-timbering of cinnamon sticks,
shingles of overlapping gingersnaps.
And the final touch—a marzipan Star

of David stuck over the chocolate bar
front door. Its six points will alert
everyone that inside is a wicked witch
who must burn to death in an oven.

Some parents deny the witch, the fire,
the blond, blue-eyed darlings who shoved
the body in, skipped home. No once upon
a time. Everyone lives happily ever after.

Say Hello to the Little Woman

She asserts herself at the damnedest times—
when they're working out at the gym, say,
or having a brandy and cigar with the boys.

It's not as if they want her to come out,
and most men manage to keep her down;
but her triumphs are many, from J. Edgar Hoover

to the boy in junior high who swung his bat
just like a girl. And you, my friend—
look how you're holding that wine glass.

The Panic Bird

just flew inside my chest. Some
days it lights inside my brain,
but today it's in my bonehouse,
rattling ribs like a birdcage.

If I saw it coming, I'd fend it
off with a machete or baseball bat.
Or grab its hackled neck,
wring it like a wet dishrag.

But it approaches from behind.
Too late I sense it at my back—
carrion, garbage, excrement.
Once inside me it preens, roosts,

vulture on a public utility pole.
Next it flaps, it cries, it glares,
it rages, it struts, it thrusts
its clacking beak into my liver,

my guts, my heart, rips off strips.
I fill with black blood, bile.
This may last minutes or days.
Then it lifts sickle-shaped wings,

rises, is gone, leaving a residue—
foul breath, droppings, molten midnight
feathers. And life continues.
And then its shadow is overhead again.

In Praise of My Prostate
(after St. Anne of Weston,
who celebrated her uterus)

My internist said you are unnaturally large.
Once chestnut-size, you've expanded, he said,
into a tennis ball. (In my encyclopedia,

you come right between Prosody and Prostitution,
just before Prosthesis—strange bedfellows.)
You are an unruly child, a real pisser.

You are a porn star who climaxes in a golden
shower. Sometimes you just peter out
in dribbles and drabs. You began when I found

blood in my semen, red curled into white,
a viscous Christmas candy cane, whirling
down the drain like blood in Hitchcock's *Psycho*.

I was certain I had the big C. "Does it burn
when you urinate?" "Never." "Do you have
trouble getting it up?" "No, my problem

is getting it down." The doctor lectured:
"Whenever you hear sounds of hooves,
the chances are it's just horses.

But if you're determined to hear a zebra,
or even a unicorn, go ahead. Be my guest."
So I thought just horses. Until I began

to drop buckets of blood, the toilet bowl
cranberry-sauce red. I was scared witless.
I got a second, and a third opinion.

To a man, they all said, "Gastroenteritis."
After weeks of expensive antibiotics,
you became healthy. A healthy horse.

Still enlarged, but no zebra, no unicorn.
I put away mortality, which I'd been lugging
around like a big battered trunk.

Now men everywhere are chanting their escapes,
celebrating their perfect little chestnuts,
perfect pelvic and spinal lymph nodes.

One is driving to Enid, Oklahoma to get married.
One is shimmying up telephone poles in Germany.
One is a perfumed gigolo in Beverly Hills.

One is a hairy son of a bitch on a cement mixer.
One attempts to teach English to Asians.
One is an Alsatian monk who vowed abstinence.

One throws pizzas over his head on Coney Island.
One implements media-software in Houston.
One is an art student working his way through college.

And one is me, saying a mantra for you—the Grand Gland.
We drive away the grackle of unhappiness.
We watch football and baseball games,

eclipses, sniff wildflowers, make love, eat
whatever we want, every meal no longer the last
for the (mistakenly) condemned man on Death Row.

No, we'll not pack our bags yet. The hooves
we shivering bastards heard were just horses.
For now, the zebras and the unicorns can wait.

Part II

Cherry Suite

She gestured toward the master bedroom suite.
"Solid cherry wood!" Mother said grandly.
Two bureaus, two mirrors, four-poster bed,
night stand, and her personal vanity.

It was the best furniture we owned.
The rest, mere veneer. Weekly she sprayed
that suite with Lemon Pledge, buffed it
till it shone deep and red as Beaujolais.

I was drawn to its many drawers, sliding
as if on casters. Hers contained paste
jewelry, perfumes, prom programs (Jefferson
High 1933, 1934), photos of her smug-faced

aviator brother, a handbag made of beads,
scarves, cosmetics, a desiccated starfish,
my stellar report cards since first grade,
an autographed photo of Miss Lillian Gish.

Besides shirts and suspenders, his held
underwear, PJs, new wallets, socks,
reeking pipes, a porno comic with a Dagwood
screwing Blondie, and under his hankies a red

and white box of Trojans: "Young Rubber Co.,
Youngstown, Ohio. Sold for the Prevention
of Disease Only." They smelled like artgum
erasers at my middle school. For comparison

I unrolled one, tried it on, despaired
I would ever fill such a thing. Ten rubbers
in the twelve-pack. The next time I looked,
only seven: Jeez, he's done it to Mother

three times in two weeks! (It never occurred
to me, they've done it three times together.)
He's crucifying her, I thought, on a cherry-
wood cross, just as I had had to bear

his cod-cold indifference. (At school
beer-breathed boys lied about sex.
I knew "nice" ladies didn't do such things.
At church Mother'd deeply genuflect,

afterward have the rector home for tea.)
Yet she seemed none the worse for wear,
warbling, "When it's springtime in the Rockies,
and the birds sing all the day," as she'd prepare

pancakes and sausages for her family of six.
Trundled across the globe to make me bourgeois,
the cherry suite's mine today—I'm orphaned.
My performance in bed? At times a faux pas.

But, I never enter that room with its bric-a-brac
without thinking, Mom, Dad, old fuckers, come back.

A Pretty Likeness of the Life

Mother in champagne-colored dress,
    neckline with navy-blue crenelles,
Father in dress-white uniform,
    their heads precisely parallel,

they face the future. "Our wedding
    portrait," Mother proudly averred.
For half a century it dominated the air
    above her cherrywood dresser.

In flattering lighting and pastels,
    they were the picture of connubiality.
Mona Lisa smile and military bearing,
    they could be in *Town and Country*.

Sorting the homeplace after both died,
    I found the individual photographs—
Mother's from a high-school prom,
    Father's a college yearbook—halves

of the composite in their bedroom.
    Friends knew they were wed by a justice
of the peace over Christmas break, but
    only I now knew it was in such a rush,

they didn't pose commemoratively.
    Later mother paid a studio to retouch
what haste and pregnancy disallowed,
    her wedding at last made illustrious.

Trashed

A college picture of Father
    in V.P.I. dress uniform
looking like young Robert Taylor,
        sat on Ellie Brownlee's dresser
since his winter break, freshman year.

He believed he truly loved her,
        sucked her lips, possessed her body.
But next year he met our mother,
        quickly married by December.
When Ellie met Mother, Ellie's a lady,

proceeded to play godmother
        to successive offspring *en masse.*
On birthdays she gave us silver dollars.
        She died single, age fifty-four.
Relatives put Dad's picture in her trash.

Found by a curious ragpicker
        who all but began to wave it,
he returned it to our front door.
        Father claimed he was quite heartsore
to learn how long Ellie'd saved it.

Family Portrait

The Prettyman's had had one done,
the Paradees and the Littletons.
It was the year everyone on "The Hill"
had a family portrait taken by Olan Mills.

Mother booked an appointment like the rest,
hustled us four into Sunday best:
Big Brother Al in tie, vested shark-
skin suit inherited from Uncle Clarke,

me in blue hand-me-down blazer (Al's),
four-in-hand tie adorned by animals,
Little Brother Burns tieless but jacketed,
three-year-old Elinor clutching Zwieback,

wearing an apple-green piqué dress,
pink rose embroidered, new from Hess's.
At Dot Layton's Beauty Salon & Emporium,
Mother's hair was permed the day before.

Now she wore a brown watered-silk number,
best gold chains, color didn't matter—
Olan Mills' photos were black and white.
Around noon mother looked benighted,

strode to the cellar stairs. With a frown
she opened the door and shouted down,
"I don't know what you're doing but it's time
you got ready. The children and I'm

about to go." "Go where?" he yelled back up.
"Oh I just knew it!" she cried, abruptly
ran to the bedroom, fell to the cherry bed.
She didn't remain there long, pled

with each of us to be still while she
brushed our hair systematically.
Unshaven, in khakis and lumberjack shirt,
Father materialized. "What the hell?" he blurted,

"Why's everyone dressed up?" "I knew
you'd forget!" she accused, "it's just like you."
She trooped her brood out like a brigadier,
and our family portrait has no father.

Letter to My Mother

You helped me pack for that milestone
event, first time away from home alone.
It didn't matter the summer camp was poor—
long on Jesus, short on funds—bordering

a tea-colored lake. No matter we could afford
only two weeks. To help get there I hoarded
months of allowances. I was ten, felt grown,
I finally was going somewhere on my own.

You folded the ironed tee-shirts and skivvies
—you even ironed and creased my dungarees.
In Southern drawl: "And of course you'll dress
for dinner!" you said, packing with the rest

my one blazer, dress shirts, and rep tie.
I didn't protest, I was an innocent stander-by.
(The suitcase was a new brown Samsonite.
Even empty that thing never was light.)

First exhilarating day—after softball, archery,
diving instruction (which I took to swimmingly)—
came rest hour. While others took a shower
or wrote postcards home, I dressed for dinner:

the white shirt, the pre-tied striped tie,
the navy jacket. In process I received a wry
glance from my counselor. The dinner bell tolled,
I felt every bit the gentleman as I strolled

toward the rustic dining room. I entered,
the room exploded with boyish hoots and laughter,
pointing at me, the funniest thing they'd seen.
They still had on their shorts or jeans.

The rest of the two weeks were impossible.
Not chosen for any teams, called a fool,
Mother, I was miserable through and through.
But when I came home I never told you.

Grandfather's Cars

Every two years he traded them in ("As soon
as the ashtrays get full," he said with good humor);
always a sedate four-door sedan, always a Buick,
always dark as the inside of a tomb.

Then one spring Grandfather took off to trade,
returned, parked proudly in the driveway.
"Shave-and-a-haircut, two bits!" blared the horn.
Grandmother emerged from the kitchen into day-

light, couldn't believe her eyes. Grandfather sat
behind the wheel of a tomato-red Lincoln
convertible, the top down. "Shave-and-a-haircut,
two bits!" "Roscoe, whatever are you thinking?"

she cried. Back into the kitchen she flew.
No matter how many times he leaned on that horn,
she wouldn't return. So he went inside,
found her decapitating strawberries with scorn.

"Katie, what's wrong with that automobile?
All my life I've wanted something sporty."
He stood there wearing his Montgomery Ward
brown suit and saddle shoes. His face was warty.

She wiped her hands along her apron,
said words that cut like a band saw:
"What ails you? They'll think you've turned fool!
All our friends are dying like flies—all!

You can't drive that thing in a funeral procession."
He knew she was right. He gave her one baleful
look, left, and returned in possession
of a four-door Dodge, black, practical as nails.

Grandfather hated that car until the day he died.

Hounds

(for Max Eberts)

When kennels traveled from all over
for a big dog show at our middle school,
I shyly gravitated toward the boxers—
regal, snaggletoothed, feisty. The *Chronicle*

next day published a picture of me
"demonstrating the breed." (Some owners
kindly allowed us kids to oversee
the competition.) I looked a connoisseur.

At home that week I began my intense campaign.
I wanted a boxer puppy for my birthday.
It was the only thing I wanted, I explained.
I'd take real good care of it, I'd say.

I'd name him Duke if he were a boy,
Duchess if she were a bitch. (A bitch!
I used the word just to annoy
Mother. She grimaced, I was in stitches.)

My birthday finally came, I raced downstairs.
"You're not ready for the responsibility,"
I was told. I fought back the tears,
drowning in injustice, a bad call from the referee.

Years passed. Then one night my beery father
came home with two basset hounds he'd won
in a poker game. I should have liked the pair,
but didn't. Squat hot dogs, hammered-down,

long floppy ears, sad watery eyes,
in no way did they resemble my beloved pet
of fantasies. "Not in my house!" Mother cried.
"They'll ruin the sofas with muddy paws, wet

all over the carpets." Father built dog houses
in the very back of the backyard, a chain-link
fence around them like convicts in a prison house
all year long. My busy father never would think

to exercise them. I totally ignored them.
Mother fed them table scraps and dry kibble.
Perhaps twice in the fall father approached the pen,
opened it and released them. What fribblery!

They howled with joy, ran in circles around the yard.
He snapped leashes on their collars, led the pair
to his car, opened the trunk, pushed them in hard.
Hansel and Gretel in the oven! Was there air?

I worried. With a wave, off he'd go to hunt.
Dick and Peggy were rabbit dogs, it turned out.
Each time father returned with unfortunate
cottontails, he'd clean them at the kitchen spout,

slitting bellies straight down the middle,
dropping blue guts and bilish black blood
into a galvanized bucket. Mother watched, I bridled.
As he skinned them raw, Father sucked on a Bud.

He forgot about the hounds soon as snow fell,
but I became their personal chargé d'affaires—
I let them out, raked their pen, made them squeal
whenever I threw a tennis ball into the air.

The next autumn, body and voice matured,
I surprised myself, accompanied Father and hounds hunting.
I winced when that fired rifle bucked my shoulder—
but shed a skin as easily as rabbits in cleaning.

All winter I hounded Mother to let them inside,
pointing out their neglect was criminal.
No, that was something she couldn't abide.
In the cold, the hounds dreamed of the coming fall.

Spinach Days

The odor of cooking spinach
brings them back: summer
evenings, the world's richest
city, Manhattan before my senior year,

when Cadillacs grew tailfins,
Buddy Holly and the Crickets alarmed
parents, Eisenhower full of wind,
Mamie tippling at the Gettysburg Farm.

A blue-chip ad agency awarded
me an "internship." I was recruited
for a world I could not afford.
In my one wash-and-wear suit,

by day I worked in a skyscraper,
aluminum waterfall a lobby construct,
rooftop restaurant for highsteppers.
I wrote clever copy: HOOVER SUCKS

for a vacuum cleaner client,
PIMPLES CAN MAKE YOU RICH!
to druggists for an astringent.
My boss rebuffed my greatest pitch,

KISS YOUR PAINFUL HEMORRHOIDS GOODBYE,
though called it a good attempt.
By night I sweated in my room at the "Y,"
non-air-conditioned, ten dollars' weekly rent.

The one window overlooked an air shaft,
but not a whisper of air shafted there.
I hung a repro of a Picasso lithograph
to make the cell less austere.

Rickety desk pushed tight against the bed,
but not so tight as my budget—
fifty-two dollars a week divided
between rent, food, books, cigarettes—

not necessarily in that order.
Even then books took precedent:
A secondhand *Sorrows of Young Werther*
at the Strand meant total absence

of lunch. Dinners I was resigned
to the Horn & Hardart Automat.
Cheap entrees revolved behind
glass doors, or the vegetable platter—

any three off the steam table
for a total of forty-five cents.
I thought spinach would enable
me with Popeye's omnipotence.

It was mushy, foul, overcooked,
the water dark as octopus ink.
For the rest, mashed potatoes, crook-
neck squash, or corn. I was delinquent

in the Great Food Chain, but content.
Near payday, no money even for spinach,
I let myself into my aunt's apartment
when she was away, quickly dispatched

whatever was in the Frigidaire,
hoping she wouldn't miss it, or
forgive. Dates were free: Washington Square,
the Cloisters, Natural History dinosaurs,

Lewisohn Stadium concerts where some wag
strung banners, EXIT IN CASE OF BRAHMS.
Summer nights strollers could zigzag
through Central Park without qualm,

or so I thought, amble through Harlem
back to the East Side, my date
swinging her handbag like a pendulum,
past laughing Negroes who'd gravitate

to front stoops. (Not for decades will
we say Blacks, then Afro-Americans,
finally African Americans. Nothing's still,
how many changes in a short life span?)

Spinach brings it back: long showers
at the "Y," simply nothing else to do,
Dark Victory billed with *Now, Voyager*
at the Thalia, monkeys at the Bronx Zoo,

browsing that smorgasbord for bibliophiles,
the Gotham, hoping to catch a rising star.
Never did, only fading James T. Farrell
imbibing at the Biltmore Men's Bar.

(The Biltmore Men's Bar! Even the name
is impossible today. But that was then.
All males, all crème de la crème,
leaned on the mahogany bar like denizens.)

I elevated atop the Empire State,
saw nothing but fog on foggy mist,
like the *White on White* immaculate
canvas at MOMA, postimpressionist;

hung outside gated Patchen Place
waiting for Cummings to cross cobbles,
or Djuna Barnes. Neither showed face.
The White Horse, where Delmore hobnobbed,

I shared a pitcher of martinis (a pitcher!)
with two older, hard-drinking pals
who were paying. I paid—a spectacular
hangover for days left me horizontal.

By August the city was a cement inferno.
My boss promised to get me away
to his family's Nantucket bungalow.
He never asked, not even by Labor Day.

One young man invited me to the Pines,
a place I'd never heard of or been.
Co-workers advised I should decline.
Instead I swam alone at the "Y," chlorine

stinging my eyes. (Stripling-shaped,
one-hundred-fifty pounds dripping wet,
the fat man inside me hadn't yet escaped.
Decades later he scored his upset.)

Hive-like corridors buzzed with queens
(no one knew the word Gays) cruising
in BVDs, one café au lait called Josephine
because of his effeminate languishing.

Locked in my oppressive room I wrote
parents dutifully, on sticky sheets
slept intermittently, dreaming anecdotes
of fame. I filled notebooks with meters,

not ads. Lines spilled like cataracts.
On occasion I wonder if I were mislead.
But most days I think I would go back.
The spinach. The loneliness. The future ahead.

Things

(for Diane Wakoski)

No ideas but in things,
said Doc Williams.
Christ! I must have
an awful lot of ideas.
God knows I have
an awful lot of things.
I never have enjoyed
the luxury of living
with nothing, even
next to nothing.
I never learned
the lesson of seeing
"isolate in the beauty
of separateness"
each thing by itself.
Unto itself, itself.

      Jay Gatsby, opening the bureau
      to display all his shirts . . .

I was planted in a crib
of things—ducks, dolls,
rattlers of the nonpoisonous
variety. Growing up I collected:
movie-star photos, baseball cards,
matchbox cars. Live things, too:
My gerbils begat unto the umpteenth
generation. College years, things
worsened. I hated library books,

still do. Worth reading,
worth owning, my motto. Bookshelves
groaned. Paper napkins? Loathe them.
Linen closets groaned. Thoreau
would groan had he seen the van
big as the Mayflower (and so named)
lumbering toward Westchester
with all my unworldly possessions.
One-hundred-ninety cartons
of books alone. No, not alone,
together.

      The Collier Brothers, leaving
      a houseful of newspapers . . .

At night I prowl the rooms
of my house, glass in hand,
to survey my things. "I'll weed
the library," I say. "Throw away
two hundred record albums"—
low-fidelity sound.
And just yesterday
they were the very thing.
Christ! I need things to keep
all my things in. And this year,
things got worse. I inherited
(of all things) Great Aunt Eva's
amber collection. Every surface
gleams—glass amber grapes,
amber apples, amber ashtrays
shaped like gentlemen's top hats.
I've had to hire a housekeeper
just to dust the damned things.

McCullers said, "First learn
to love a tree, a rock, a cloud . . . "

I do, I do. I love shoe
trees, rock records, Rolls-Royce
Silver Clouds. Lord, help me
abandon these screens I stand
behind. Help me come to believe,
no things but in ideas.

603 Cross River Road
(for Judith)

1972: The Land—A Love Letter

This hill and the old house on it
are all we have. Two acres
more or less—half crabby lawn,
half field we mow but twice a year.

Some trees we planted, most gifts
of the land. The pine by the kitchen?
Grown twice as fast as our son. The bald
elm lost the race with my hairline.

The mulberry—so lively with squirrels,
chipmunk chases, and songbirds—
fell like a tower in the hurricane.
My chainsaw ate fruitwood for weeks.

(I stacked the heavy logs by the cellar
door, to be retrieved winter nights
for the fireplace, not knowing it's easier
to burn a cement block than a mulberry.)

The juniper tree, the one that all but
obliterated our view? Men cut it down
to make way for the new well and water
pump. That pump should pump pure gold:

we lay awake engineering ways to get it
paid for. But we'll never leave
this mortgaged hill, we thought.
This land is changing as we change,

its face erodes like ours—weather marks,
stretch marks, traumas of all sorts
and conditions. Last night a limb broke
in the storm. We still see it limn the sky.

Wife, we've become where we have been.
This land is all we have, but this love
letter is no more ours than anyone's
who ever married the land . . .

1982: Autumn Crocuses

Basketing leaves during earth's
annual leavetaking, we've realized
with a start—something's missing.
The autumn crocuses that would spring

each October by these rocks.
No longer here! We never planted them,
but they implanted themselves
on us. Now, for their lack

we are poorer. Purest orchid color,
they astonished amidst the season's
dwindling. Crocus in autumn?
How perverse, to reverse the seasons.

Every year we bore a bouquet
into the house with pride,
surprising guests who'd never seen
their like. They thought them

foreign, remote, inaccessible—
like edelweiss. No vase, glass, or jar
ever contained them. Their soft white
stems always bent, jack-eared blossoms

lolled like heads of old folks
sleeping in rocking chairs.
I read once where their yellow pistils
are a saffron source. For us,

source of satisfaction. Now gone.
A woodchuck? Frost? My failure to care
for bulbs? They were the unaccountable
we thought we could count on.

1992: Farewell to the Blue House

Our favorite time of year was fall.
Autumn crocuses had blazed
in rock gardens like gas flames,
trees painted themselves pumpkin,
apple, fireplace smoke traveled

in the breezes. The fall of leaves
created a cinematic panorama—
the spangled lake blue, bluer
than blue beneath Westchester's
skies. Mornings, Canada geese

vectored down, honking and hunkering
in the lower field. Evenings, deer
leapt stone walls, drank their fill.
In the upper field, wild turkeys
strutted. The peaceable kingdom.

Whenever I tired of the city,
I lost myself in trees.
Whenever I tired of human faces,
I bent down sunflowers,
gazed into friendly countenances.

The sun setting over the reservoir,
orange overcoming bruise-colored clouds—
no one felt luckier to have landed somewhere.
Somedays I felt as if I could walk across that water.

Part III

Sunday Driver

I was a Sunday driver, cruising
along life's superhighway,
neck craned left, then right,
in anticipation of accidents.
In a 70-mile-an-hour zone,
I ventured 50. Then I stalled.

And next you raced up, topless
in your little sky-blue sports car,
looking cute. "Hop in," you said.
I abandoned my sedate sedan
on the shoulder without
even turning on the blinkers.

I sit next to you and four-
on-the-floor. "Life in the fast
lane, Kid," you say and laugh.
The car spins out deliriously.
Wind whips my silver hair.

No Thanksgiving

Congratulations on your new house!
There will probably be no poem
commemorating this happy event,
as you are a bitter poet. I imagine
your disappointment when something nice
happens to you: no poem comes out of it.
    –Letter from Adam Zagajewski to R. P.

For her winsome, angular face
that crinkles with smiles,
I'll give no thanksgiving.

Nor will I write about her body,
"white as a white cow's milk,"
which greatly turns me on.

No word for slight shoulders
that lean into me whenever
I need comfort or support.

No poem in praise of hands
that habitually clasp mine
with unexpected strength.

No celebration of breasts
fleshly pomegranates,
just as tart to the tongue.

No panegyric for pubic hair,
brown, curly, crisp,
tantalizingly textural.

No lauds for the miraculous
surprise when she kissed
me for the first time.

Nor will I express gratitude
for her humor, making me
laugh even when apart.

No jubilee for that accident
which brought us together
so many years ago.

I won't even bless her
words—fugues, counterpoints,
extended and intricate as Bach's.

No. I'm pegged as a poet
of wormwood and gall. I won't
tempt Fate expressing such love.

The Changed Man

If you were to hear me imitating Pavarotti
in the shower every morning, you'd know
how much you have changed my life.

If you were to see me stride across the park,
waving to strangers, then you would know
I am a changed man—like Scrooge

awakened from his bad dreams feeling feather-
light, angel-happy, laughing the father
of a long line of bright laughs—

"It is still not too late to change my life!"
It is changed. Me, who felt short-changed.
Because of you I no longer hate my body.

Because of you I buy new clothes.
Because of you I'm a warrior of joy.
Because of you and me. Drop by

this Saturday morning and discover me
fiercely pulling weeds gladly, dedicated
as a born-again gardener.

Drop by on Sunday—I'll Turtlewax
your sky-blue sports car, no sweat. I'll greet
enemies with a handshake, forgive debtors

with a papal largesse. It's all because
of you. Because of you and me,
I've become one changed man.

Oysters

One evening we toasted with whiskey sours
below Grand Central, in the Oyster Bar.
We sat at the rail, felt the world was ours.

We ordered some of every kind there are—
the Chincoteague, Box, Cotuit, Wellfleet . . .
You called their looks slimy, just like catarrh.

I quoted the poet, sounding effete:
"Oh, it was a brave man who first ate one!"
Feeling brave, we proceeded to eat.

We compared sizes, colors, con-
sistencies, all the nuances lovers
can extract from moments of pure fun.

Some we squirted with lime, some we covered
with horseradish or Tabasco. A few,
too salty, we sentenced to be smothered

in chilled cocktail sauce. With great ado
that night I showed you—the novice—the way
to act Mrs. Waters. You took my cue,

raised an oyster high overhead, in play
opened your mouth wide as the gates of hell,
and sucked all the mollusk's juices away.

Darling, you learned that lesson much too well.
You took my copious feast, dumped the shell.

What's the Point?

It could be the index hand of a clock, creating
the trite expression, "At this point in time."

It could be a green dot in an impressionist painting,
which eyes create with yellow and blue.

It could be the muzzle of a dog, stretched rigidly
toward the game, one paw raised.

It could be the tip of a veterinarian's needle,
plunged into a cat's ninth life.

It could be a decimal mistake, created by a computer,
making someone a millionaire. For a day.

It could be the end of the horn of a snail,
rapidly withdrawn in sensitivity.

It could be a flower's pistil which fascinates
hairy-legged aliens with four wings.

It could be a tiny deer-tick bite. Unnoticed,
its consequences are considerable.

It could be a glowing spot on the x-ray
of my lung—a much-delayed annual checkup.

It could be a vector of an airplane I almost missed,
which now for the life of me I cannot get off.

It could be a point of honor, on which you acted
(if I may say so) over-fastidiously.

It may be the point in question, wrong-headedly
    entered on both our agendas.

It might be your unexpected point of departure.
    Without you, life is pointless.

Fifth Season
(after a line by Yvon Goll)

Please return. I shall invent
a fifth season for us.
Dogs will fly, cats will play
violins, silver lavalieres
will ripen like fruit on trees.
The sky's chartreuse,
grass lavender as lilacs,

just as fragrant. By day
there will be two moons.
The words you used to say
goodbye will disappear
from the lexicon. The airport
from which you flew
will dissolve to cinders.

Simply return, do.
I will grow younger,
you never will grow older,
we will inhabit a garden
of unearthly possibilities
where the clock never strikes,
it never becomes midnight.

Epistles
(Three Somonkas)

i.

You ask how many
kisses would satisfy me?
Count all the sand grains
on the beach, all the night stars—
their number might satisfy.

All the grains of sand,
and all the heavenly stars,
   would not be enough
to satiate me, my dear.
You must think infinitely.

ii.

I cannot tell you
how much last night meant to me.
No one has made love
to me with so much passion.
I count the days till next week.

This is just to say
we won't be meeting again.
   You're nothing in bed,
and a man needs his loving.
Please return my ring by mail.

iii.

I am writing you
from my room in the tower.

I cannot write poems
anymore, I've said it all.
Why don't you come or write me?

Sorry for neglect.
Much too busy writing love
poems to come visit.
I have a new muse named Bea.
Perhaps you should get a dog?

The Pillsbury Doughboy Is Alive and Well in Ohio

This is just to say the man who looks
like the Pillsbury Doughboy has cut out.
He decided he's from a different mold.

When last seen the Pillsbury Doughboy
was not jogging, was mooning around
a Manhattan cocktail party where only assorted
raw vegetables were served; everyone drank
Perrier water and quoted the duchess of Windsor,
"You can never be too thin or too rich."

This is just to say
the Pillsbury Doughboy grew sick
of insinuations about his weight,
resented no one wanting to sit next to him
on airplanes, is through trying to fit
into "European Cut" shirts and jackets
(cut for scrawny little Frenchmen),
grew weary of skinny women jabbing a finger
into his tummy, expecting him to giggle on cue.

Now rumor has it
the Pillsbury Doughboy works in a bakery
somewhere in Ohio (that fat-cat state
that begins with an O and ends with an O).
He produces white bread dazzlingly white.
It is not unbleached. It is not stone-ground.
It is full of artificial preservatives.
It is unregenerately unenriched.

When you read this,
you will know the Pillsbury Doughboy is happy.
For lunch he eats greasy french fries every day.
After work he eats heavy cookies from the bakery,
drinks milk which tastes, almost, like milk
he had as a farm boy: It has not been protein-
fortified. It has not had vitamins A and D
added. It is not, certainly, low-fat. It is milk.

Every night he goes to a sleazy nightclub,
drinks beer out of longnecks. The beer is not Lite.
The blue lights make his complexion look less doughy.
He sits there entranced, listening to
the Gingerbread Lady sing sweet songs.
Her eyes are raisins, her mouth a cherry.
Even her voice is full of calories.

Someday the Pillsbury Doughboy
will run off with the Gingerbread Lady.
They will live on Lollipop Lane in a little
gingerbread house. And one day, he will eat her
right up if she doesn't watch out.

John Dillinger's Dick

Some say it's pickled
(formaldehyde) in the basement
of a funeral parlor in Indiana.
Some say the mortician
had heard of Dillinger's
legendary endowment—
the gangster's gun molls
and cell mates talked.
When the corpse was delivered
by the F.B.I., the undertaker
couldn't wait for the stiff's
great unveiling. He wasn't
interested in bullet holes
(one in the face was
a matter for makeup).
He undertook to measure
length, circumference:
Even nontumescent
it was monumental.
Why should such a marvel
be buried? The mortician,
with his wife's boning knife,
carved away his fleshly
trophy. No one would know:
When laid out in his coffin
the gangster wore a suit.
Some nights as his wife
slept, the undertaker crept down

to the basement, removed
the red velvet cloth
covering the pickle jar,
switched on the lamp—
the jar brilliantly backlit—
and sat admiring.
A few times he invited
his fellow morticians
to come view his jar.
They joked, speculated
what woman could accommodate
it all. Some days he wished
he'd taken the balls too.
Against all offers,
he wouldn't part
with Dillinger's private part.
Since 1934 it's floated
and danced in its memorial
waters, lifting its great
uncircumcised head, mooning
against the glass. When
will it rise again, source
of so much pleasure
and pain? It was like
Albert Einstein's extracted
brain, said to be dropped
by some doltish technician—
splattered and shattered
on the laboratory floor
before it, too, properly
could be measured. But
no measure in death would do
for such prodigious organs.

Only in life, only in action,
could they reveal all
their awesome capability.

Sonata

I. When You Massage

my back, Love, heaven is in your hands,
healing with your touch.

When you work my back, tightness slackens,
cares dissolve, muscles

unkink. I am one with the sea's cadence,
the earth's revolution,

the heart's engine. You knead me, I need you,
sensual as silk, all flesh

is grass, mine rippling waves of wild grass.
You cure me by caring.

II. "You're Coming Unglued,"

a true friend confided. I replied that,
like a formerly solid antique table,
I was experiencing a certain detachment,

a certain separation, a certain desiccation
at solid joinings that had supported me.
It's not as if I willed it. The climate

in which I find myself was unexpectedly
unfriendly. Given so much heat,
nothing could maintain its integrity.

III. After the Crash

they laid out the wreckage of our disaster,
our love affair, in a cavernous airline hangar.
Experts recovered thousands of discrete pieces,
sonar scans sweeping across the creases
of the ocean bed, hoping to uncover
the source of what went wrong, to discover
a missile, a bomb, mechanical failure, human error.
There were no survivors.

Personals

I'm honest, discreet, and no way a lech.
Staying home with a rented video is just fine.
I'm seeking a friend first, we'll see what happens next.

My definition of fun is not very far-fetched:
Enjoy fishing, four-wheeling, casinos, and wine.
I'm honest, discreet, and no way a lech.

Want face-to-face conversation, no phone sex,
Non-smoking, drug-free women—the old-fashioned kind.
I'm seeking a friend first, we'll see what happens next.

I like a lady to let her hair down, get a little wrecked.
I have brown hair, brown eyes, am built along trim lines.
I'm honest, discreet, and no way a lech.

I'm thirty-seven, white, have two teenagers by my ex.
Looking for a lady, any age or race, similarly inclined.
I'm seeking a friend first, we'll see what happens next.

No psychos! (My ex didn't play with a full deck.)
I live on the northwest side, near the refinery.
I'm honest, discreet, and no way a lech.
I'm seeking a friend first. We'll see what happens next.

Never Date Yourself
(remark by Rob House)

Why not? It increases your chances for a date
on Saturday nights. I'd called every unfortunate

in town, been shot down. So finally I telephoned
myself on my own phone mail, left a high-toned

message: I'd be picking myself up at 8:15.
Took a long shower, struggled into Calvin Klein jeans.

Next Ralph Lauren sport coat, Gucci loafers, no sox.
Reeking of Chanel for Men, I felt quite cocksure.

I dropped the Corvette top, drove us to Cinema II.
Ironically, a double feature, both Gerard Depardieu.

Bought us a popcorn dripping with extra butter,
we dived in with both hands, busy as a knitter.

In the dark my left hand held my right,
one thigh touched the other, just slightly.

Between features I had to go to the john.
In the aisle I glanced back, saw me seated alone.

After the show, paused for a smoke in the lot.
Myself lit my cigarette. It was almost erotic.

Then a fern bar filled with Yuppie scum.
We drank double Dewars, Tweedledee, Tweedledum,

resisted urges to pilot us to the dance
floor. Others doubtless would look askance.

Back home I slowly undressed, just one kiss
on the mouth in the bedroom mirror, dismissed

making love to myself in the looking glass.
(I'm not that kind of guy—I've got more class,

it was only our first date, there's time.)
Next day I leave myself a message: "I'm

glad we went out. I had a ball.
In this postmodern age, everyone dates it all."

Sex

Whenever I have it, I'm never in bed
with just my partner. Parents attend,
tsk-tsking under the sheets. Freud
takes notes at the footboard. Jane Russell,
looking just as she did in *The Outlaw*,
squeezes in, Brobdignagian boobs
for my pillows. Harry Reams sidles up,
crowing about his studlier performances.
Kinsey perches on the headboard, calculator
in hand. The seventh grade teacher
for whom I burned and itched comes,
still patronizing. A junior high cheer-
leader, bouncing on the mattress, sis-boom-
bahs my every position. A neighbor who hangs
black Victoria's Secret undies on the line
is back-to-back. Margaret Mead observes.
Lorena Bobbitt lies spoon-fashion and has
her knife. A high school linebacker
who patted my uniformed butt and barked,
"Nice game, Bobby!" cuddles close, confusing
me. Jerry Springer is videotaping
my grunts and heaves for national TV.
It gets very crowded. It's enough to take
the lead out of a Fort Ticonderoga pencil.

The Man Who Fell in Love with His Cat

There was a man who fell in love with his cat.
He didn't intend to fall in love with his cat.
It was a nice cat, but he'd had lots of cats.
At first she seemed to belong to his daughter,

but his daughter went away to college. His wife went
away to a separate bedroom. One night he woke
in the middle of the night and found his cat
lying beside him, her head on his shoulder.

This went on for some time, and his daughter stayed
away at college and his wife stayed away
in her separate bed, and he kept discovering
this cat beside him, head on his shoulder.

One day he decided to take the cat for a ride.
He didn't put her in the cat carrier, too
unfriendly considering their relationship.
She purred on the front seat, head in his lap.

They drove through housing developments,
through grounds of an elementary school,
gardens of a historical estate. That night
she lay in his bed, head on his shoulder.

Soon he was taking her to the cinemaplex,
a Chinese restaurant, even to his office
in the city, where she lay in a stupor all day.
Office workers never questioned the cat.

On the train she leaned her head on his shoulder.
Commuter and conductors never asked why
he traveled with a cat with her head on his shoulder.
Through Grand Central she followed him like a dog.

Sometimes she sat on his head like a coonskin cap.
Or wrapped herself around his neck like a scarf.
Or hung over his wrists like a fur muff in winter.
Whatever it was she needed, he was there.

One night he came home from a business trip
(it didn't seem practical to take the cat to Chicago).
When he looked for her she was nowhere.
He thought he detected blood spots on the living room

carpet, but wasn't sure. His wife said
the cat had shot out the door when she took out
the garbage, and she never came back.
His wife leaned her head on his shoulder.

And they were sleeping together ever since,
until one morning he awoke, his wife was cold.
The doctor said he hadn't seen anything like it:
Her eyes seemed to have been scratched out.

The man wondered about his wife's fate,
about his own fate. Then later that night,
as he was settling into insomnia, he shifted
and felt, on his shoulder, the head of the cat.

Part IV

Found Poems

i.

(from a letter by Emily Dickinson)

When you wrote
you would come in November
it would please me
it was November then—but the time
has moved. You went
with the coming of the birds—they will go
with your coming,
but to see you is so much sweeter than birds,
I could excuse the spring . . .
Will you come in November, and will November
come, or is this the hope that opens
and shuts like the eyes of the wax doll?

ii.

(from a letter by Gerard Manley Hopkins)

The only just judge,
the only just literary critic,
is Christ,

who prizes, is proud of,
and admires, more than
any man,

more than the receiver himself
can, the gifts of
his own making.

iii.

(from a letter by Katherine Mansfield)

Dear Princess Bibesco,
I am afraid you must stop
writing these little love letters
to my husband while he and I
live together. It is one of the things
which is not done in our world.

You are very young. Won't you ask
your husband to explain to you
the impossibility of such a situation?
Please do not make me write to you
again. I do not like scolding people
and hate having to teach them manners.

iv.

(from a letter by Vincent Van Gogh)

I think that I still have it
in my heart someday
to paint a bookshop
with the front yellow and pink,
in the evening, and the black
passerby like a light
in the midst of darkness.

The Uses of Not

Hollowed out,
clay makes a pot.
Where pot's not
is where it's useful.
–Lao Tzu, *Tao Te Ching*
    (translated by LeGuin)

When I'm doing nothing
is when I'm most
productive. The mind
empty as a pot
begins to fill—
images, ideas, plots.

Air travel is ideal.
Strapped next to strangers,
unoccupied for hours,
simply have a drink
and think. The note
book begins to fill.

Hotel rooms work well.
Sniffling air conditioner,
a bed, a chair, a desk—
and only me, lonely
as a figure in a Hopper.
Perfect for writing.

Late Reading

(April 20, 1966)

Omissions are not errors.
–Marianne Moore,
 Preface to *Collected Poems*

Admiring her work and enjoying
a correspondence (she pronounced
in minuscule of one of my modest
poems, "All lines so veracious!")

we traveled to Washington Square
where she was to read at NYU.
Our expectations were elevated:
She'd be witty, wear her tricorn hat.

It was a frail old woman mounted
the platform slowly, bare of head,
wearing pink and white calico.
Her voice gossamer, she read

terribly, swallowing whole lines,
skipping entire stanzas. These
omissions were errors, the poems
mutilated before a wincing public.

Afterward we queued with students
to shake her hand. When she saw
us with her *Arctic Ox* she chortled,
"My favorite of all!", inscribed it

"For Bob and Judy," but forgot to sign
her name. It was a day of blunders;
a great hitter was striking out.
We left, fans whose home team lost.

It was six more years before she died,
that fabricator of frigate pelicans,
pangolins, sea unicorns, steeple-jacks,
plumet basilisks, paper nautiluses.

But reader, there is no stumbling
on her pages. On the bookshelf
her poems tick like quartz crystals,
precise as the world's exactest clock.

Homage to a Nonagenarian
(for Stanley Kunitz)

The white tern lays a single egg,
in an act of frail balance,
within a fork or on a horizontal
branch. A marvel the elements
don't bring it smithereening down.

After the chick hatches, it clings
to the limb with wide webbed feet.
In rain, in wind, it cleaves, nods,
surviving against the odds.
Like you, old friend, who hangs on.

Fort Juniper Annual Thanksgiving Day Family Gathering
(in memoriam: R. F.)

The round black walnut dining table
is set for a vegetarian feast for eight:
baked soybeans in cheese sauce,
tossed lettuce salad, homemade brown bread,
creamed potatoes with fresh parsley,
wild grape jam fresh from the vine,
a bottle of homemade elderflower wine.

Both maternal and paternal grandparents,
mother and father, sister Ida May,
all are there when host Robert Francis
sits down, unfolds his napkin, says
grace before all the framed photographs
he placed around that tabletop,
before the seven empty chairs.

Gifts

Are the best gifts the gifts
you would give yourself?

Perhaps. Better, the best gifts
are those which are the self.

Carson knew. One blue day
she gave Tennessee a china set,

Irish Belleek. Today only
a pitcher and a cup remain.

Carson and the chinaware:
Both too fragile to last.

Instrument of Choice

She was a girl
no one ever chose
for teams or clubs,
dances or dates,

so she chose the instrument
no one else wanted:
the tuba. Big as herself,
heavy as her heart,

its golden tubes
and coils encircled her
like a lover's embrace.
Its body pressed on hers.

Into its mouthpiece she blew
life, its deep-throated
oompahs, oompahs sounding,
almost, like mating cries.

Brother Francis and Brother Wolf
(for Samuel B. Southwell)

We've heard about his sermons to the birds,
which many dismissed as totally absurd.
The birds proved his meaning was not lost,
by flying away in the formation of a cross.

But who has heard about his conversion
of wild animals? Gubbio was overrun
by wolves ravening the streets,
making citizens and livestock dead meat.

Francis journeyed there, cried out, "Brother
Wolf, come show yourself! We together
must reason!" And the powerful pack leader
approached Francis, brother to brother.

Francis was fearless, stroked the dense fur.
Feral jaws relaxed, the fierce cur
knelt at his feet. The Franciscan preached,
filling the creature with something like peace:

"Brother Sun, Sister Moon, Brother Wind,
and Sister Water are one," the Franciscan said.
"All nature is the mirror of our God,
we must love one another and be good."

The Wolf remembered things he never knew
he knew, and taking lead, his pack withdrew.
Those brothers never attacked Gubbio again.
Francis returned to preaching to the wrens.

Song for an Infant Son
(for Graham)

Baby bunting, my guru,
    may you always wish to hunt
the lively, the choice, the true.

May your eyes, so wise and googly,
    escape "sophistication,"
retain their innocent hue.

May your laugh quicksilver
    the wind when you
realize your sweetest plans.

May you find someone to love
    spontaneous as lightning;
you'll know what I am speaking of.

Houston Haiku

i.

Dusk. Fireflies are gold
teeth in a gospel singer's
palatial mouth.

ii.

So ethereal,
       music of Claude Debussy—
perfume for the ear.

iii.

Pocked-mocked old pervert,
       the moon, lurks behind hedges
looking for lovers.

iv.

The night she first kissed
       his mouth, he was pleased as
a dog with two tails.

v.

Her silicon breasts:
       round, firm, golden, as ersatz
as canned Cling peach halves.

vi.

Trying to love her
       is just like licking honey
from the razor's edge

vii.

Talk about the past:
      a cat explaining how to
descend a ladder.

viii.

The frozen rain drop,
      dozing on the death-black twig,
dreams of hurricanes.

Gout

It starts with a major invasion
    south, at the peninsula's tip.
The buildup continues, advancing ganglions,
    swelling their bloody bagpipes.

Infantrymen move toward the head.
    They volley rubicund vortices.
The fiery foothold is impeded,
    the resistance brought to its knees.

For the wounded and hostaged, no retreat—
    their pain tighter than piano wire.
No anguish like the anguish of the defeated.
    Avoid at all costs being taken prisoner.

Two for Amy Jones

I. A Painting

You placed this bouquet upon the waters.
    Casual flowers meant to cheer. Childhood colors:
pink, yellow, green, blue. Loveable, touching. A starfall.

It is a bridal bouquet tossed away in ecstasy.
    It is a floral tribute never delivered to a talent.
It exists upon a plane beyond ecstasy and talent.

See how it is wrapped in newspaper, floating.
    See how it has nothing to do with news, floating.
See how it is neither above or below, real or unreal.

Surely it is rooted, this bouquet of cut flowers,
    in the feminine soul. But—and don't miss it—
a sailboat. Small, white, it floats just beyond:

the male force billowing and blossoming. Bouquet and boat,
    uniting opposites within the celestial light shining,
within the biggest flower's magical black eye.

Look into the eye of the flower, into the eye
    of God, the I of God. Bouquet and boat, flower and I,
real and unreal, male and female, all have become one.

II. An Eclogue

To reach your peeling, pillared house,
one went down wooded Sorrel Road,
(I'd misheard it as "Sorrow Road." Since then,
I've read, in parts of England, sorrel
is called sorrow). Nothing sorrowful

about you or your home. You hustled about,
begonias and cabbage roses in profusion,
ancestral silver tea service twinkling.
One of your small luxuries, you paid a maid
to keep it shining. Your pink, orange, blue

paintings—Piazza San Marco, Duomo with flags flying,
Venetian cats circling alfresco tables like sharks—
were on every wall, stacked in the hall.
Pictures weren't all you painted. Annually
you'd Jackson Pollock the wooden floors,

vivid dribbles, swirls atop battleship grey.
For a brush you used a chicken feather:
"Nothing but a chicken feather achieves
this delicate effect," you crowed. Your Italianisms
glittered like your service—

risi e bisi, pinot grigio, pensione, bienale . . .
And how you loved word play! One oil painting
(brassieres flapping on an Italian clothesline)
became titularly, "The Nipples of Naples." You were
a slightly naughty teenager, no octogenarian.

After dark you engaged in drink. "More vino,
Dearie?" you'd ask, helping yourself liberally,
or to a gin martini. Small, you were elfin—
hair dyed chestnut, brocade ballet slippers,
shocking pink or kelly green thrift-shop frocks.

Sympathetic, generous, you surprised me
the way you abused your cat. Thin tabby, female,
loving, you never allowed her into the house,
even in icicle weather. When you went abroad,
no provisions. "She'll catch mice or birds,"

you reassured. You had several husbands, cast out
like cats, and one septuagenarian patrician boy-
friend. Driving you to an event, he argued
over politics, so you popped out of his Mercedes,
trudged home in evening gown in the snow.

Once at a dinner party for eight, you produced
a small chicken, asked me to carve. I quartered it,
sent four plates down the table, asked for the
second chicken. There was none. Retrieving plates,
embarrassedly recarving, I reapportioned.

You painted every day, etched caped Ezra Pound,
cast a bronze bust of Marianne Moore, your idol.
You never abandoned Italian lessons, returned
to Venice whenever a major painting was sold,
refreshing your sense of your special world.

Until you began to fall. First, face down
on Tarrytown Library's stone steps. Next, catching
your heel, a wrought-iron patio chair leg—
breaking your eyeglasses but not your hip.
Your California daughter, concerned, sold your house,

transported you to Escondido, Juniper Street.
I thought Juniper boded well—flourishing
evergreen of your native Northeast, flavoring
in your gin. Your daughter's house
was just across the way. She always looked in.

You set up studio, began to paint an alien
western landscape. Not for long. Your mind drifted,
a bad radio signal—classical shifting to rock.
Books went unread, paintings begun, unfinished.
You entered hospital, never checked out.

Your work not sought now, your New York dealer defunct,
for old time's sake I drive down Sorrel Road.
The rustic road sign should surely be changed.
With you not there, Sorrel transliterates into Sorrow.

Compartments

Which shall be final?
      Pine box in a concrete vault,
urn on a mantel?

Last breath a rattle,
      stuffed in a black body bag,
he's zipped head to toe.

At the nursing home,
      sides drawn to prevent a fall,
in a crib again.

His dead wife's false teeth
      underfoot in their bedroom.
Feel the piercing chill!

Pink flamingo lawn,
      a Florida trailer park:
one space he'll avoid.

The box they gave him
      on retirement held a watch
that measures decades.

The new bifocals
      rest in their satin-lined case,
his body coffined.

Once he was pink-slipped.
      Dad helped out: "A son's a son,
Son, from womb to tomb."

Move to the suburbs.
 Crowded train at 7:02,
empty head at night.

New playpen, new crib,
 can't compete with the newness
of the newborn child.

Oak four-poster bed
 inherited from family—
Jack Frost defrosted.

Fourteen-foot ceilings,
 parquet floors, marble fireplace,
proud first apartment.

The Jack Frost Motel,
 the very name a portent
for their honeymoon.

Backseat of a car,
 cursing the inventor of
nylon pantyhose.

First-job cubicle—
 just how many years before
a window office?

College quad at noon,
 chapel bells, frat men, coeds,
no pocket money.

His grandfather's barn.
 After it burned to the ground,
the moon filled its space.

His favorite tree—
        the leaves return to branches?
No, butterflies light.

Closet where he hid
        to play with himself. None knew?
Mothball orgasms.

Chimney that he scaled
        naked, to sweep for his dad:
Blake's soot-black urchin.

The town swimming pool
        instructor, throwing him in
again and again . . .

Kindergarten play
        -ground: swings, slides, rings, jungle gym.
Scraped knee, molester.

Red, blue, and green birds
        mobilize over his crib,
its sides a tall fence.

Two months' premature,
        he incubates by lightbulbs
like a baby chick.

He is impatient,
        curled in fetal position,
floating in darkness.

ROBERT PHILLIPS is author of five previous books of poetry, most recently *Breakdown Lane* (Johns Hopkins University Press, 1994), which the *New York Times Book Review* named a Notable Book of the Year and which was also runner-up for the Poets' Prize. For twenty-five years Phillips ran the renowned poetry reading series at the Katonah Village Library in Westchester County, New York. He now is poetry editor of the *Texas Review* and a councilor of the Texas Institute of Letters. His honors include the Award in Literature from the American Academy of Arts and Letters. He teaches at the University of Houston, where he has been director of the Creative Writing Program and now is a John and Rebecca Moores Scholar.

Poetry Titles in the Series

John Hollander, *"Blue Wine" and Other Poems*
Robert Pack, *Waking to My Name: New and Selected Poems*
Philip Dacey, *The Boy under the Bed*
Wyatt Prunty, *The Times Between*
Barry Spacks, *Spacks Street: New and Selected Poems*
Gibbons Ruark, *Keeping Company*
David St. John, *Hush*
Wyatt Prunty, *What Women Know, What Men Believe*
Adrien Stoutenberg, *Land of Superior Mirages: New and Selected Poems*
John Hollander, *In Time and Place*
Charles Martin, *Steal the Bacon*
John Bricuth, *The Heisenberg Variations*
Tom Disch, *Yes, Let's: New and Selected Poems*
Wyatt Prunty, *Balance as Belief*
Tom Disch, *Dark Verses and Light*
Thomas Carper, *Fiddle Lane*
Emily Grosholz, *Eden*
X. J. Kennedy, *Dark Horses*
Wyatt Prunty, *The Run of the House*
Robert Phillips, *Breakdown Lane*
Vicki Hearne, *The Parts of Light*
Timothy Steele, *The Color Wheel*
Josephine Jacobsen, *In the Crevice of Time: New and Collected Poems*
Thomas Carper, *From Nature*
John Burt, *Work without Hope*
Charles Martin, *What the Darkness Proposes*
Wyatt Prunty, *Since the Noon Mail Stopped*
William Jay Smith, *The World Below the Window: Poems, 1937-1997*
Wyatt Prunty, *Unarmed and Dangerous: New and Selected Poems*
Robert Phillips, *Spinach Days*

Library of Congress Cataloging-in-Publication Data

Phillips, Robert S.
     Spinach days : poems / by Robert Phillips.
          p.   cm. — (Johns Hopkins, poetry and fiction)
     ISBN 0-8018-6451-8 (acid-free paper)
     I. Title.   II. Series.

PS3566.H5 S65 2000
811'.54—dc21   99-057067